Also by James McMichael

POETRY

Against the Falling Evil

The Lover's Familiar

Four Good Things

Each in a Place Apart

The World at Large: New and Selected Poems, 1971–1996

Capacity

NONFICTION

The Style of the Short Poem

"Ulysses" and Justice

If You Can Tell

Farrar, Straus and Giroux

New York

If You Can Tell

James McMichael

Farrar, Straus and Giroux

18 West 18th Street, New York 10011

Copyright © 2016 by James McMichael

All rights reserved
First edition, 2016

Library of Congress Cataloging-in-Publication Data

McMichael, James, 1939–

[Poems. Selections]

If you can tell / James McMichael. — First edition.

pages ; cm

ISBN 978-0-374-17518-4 (hardcover) — ISBN 978-0-374-71490-1 (e-book)

I. Title.

PS3563.A31894 A6 2016

811'.54—dc23

2015022218

Designed by Quemadura
www.fsgbooks.com
www.twitter.com/fsgbooks
www.facebook.com/fsgbooks

10 9 8 7 6 5 4 3 2 1

Susan

Contents

If You Can Tell

The Believed In

Christmas comes from stories.
These promise that God's love for us will outstrip death.
Only if it's not likely to can the believed in happen.
All I can be sure of waiting for it
is that I want it to come. I'd rather it be

love that at its last the body can't

take anymore and dies of,
alive at once to its having been made good.
Results at the end vary. Children beloved by them
are sometimes told by the dying

"I thought it would be you of
all people who would keep me here."
If it's to be to God's keep that I give up those I lose,

then God both knew what it was to lose a son and could do
nothing either time to save him.

That doesn't sound like God. I'm supposing God can do all.
Lost twice to body, Jesus was as quickly back again in
God's love forever.
It was given to me to have been

loved for my first six years in a house that had my nanny
Florence in it and my mother and dad. Never talked about
even by them,
my mother's doom was there too. In the looks those three passed,
each had to have seen the stakes in who was who

and may have wanted to switch.

I'm lost to the ways that love is right
at bodies sometimes, always just as it's leaving and
often without touch.

Exchange

I answer the phone.
After the usual delay,
no telemarketing hum but a male-voiced

"Gotcha,

gotcha a little bit."
His tone is practiced.
It boasts he's finalized
everything that needed saying.
Here in me to be jeered at is the thing we've

all got coming that may not end well.
I hang up
gotten a little,
go back to being gettable,

on call.
(Two months ago I deferred jury duty.

A machine will tell me soon I'm wanted in court.)

It's projected that in not many years
there will be fewer of us
dead than alive. All of us,
so far,

are either
dead or on call.
He didn't know me from Adam.
He learned from my "Hello" that I wanted him to be
heard from. He obliged.

Heard Said

I'm four
at the hospital I was born in.
From behind the nurse's
white gown and mask:

I want you to count backward from

ten for me now
out loud.

*

My stepmother
with a stack of my father's papers.
What do I
do with it,
Jimmie?

*

It was a beautiful suit of clothes,
very expensive.
I saw it hanging from the mirror

on the far side of his car.
He was so pleased

when he found my note on the windshield.
He took the suit upstairs
and came back down
to let me see it on him.

*

When they want rain,

they put their mouths to the water and blow.
They take some in their hands
and as they throw it upward cry
Look here!
Do like this!

*

A note to her
television set
was left by a woman

who then took her own life.

*

We were replaced on the line by the Unimates.
They're good at the work. They're never late. The one
problem with them is that they
don't buy cars.

*

It defies me.
I put it right here where I
always do,
and it's not there.
I loathe a beastly key.

*

If you work hard to keep a secret,
you're resentful when it's not found out.

*

Through our closed
eyelids as the bomb exploded,
we could see every bone in our hands.

*

It has a Slavic name he couldn't pronounce. I said
It's flanged and chrome,
with seven spiders on each side.
That's it, he said. Where can he buy it,

he needs it today. I told him
I don't know, but I've got one in my garage.

*

She can't leave you alone.
Sits you down,
feeds you what you don't need to eat.
It's no use telling Bertie Mae no.
And of course we wouldn't take nothing for her.

*

I've killed other people.
You'll find that this will go better
if you and I don't talk.

*

Foreplay starts at breakfast.

*

On the answering machine:
If you could

call me tonight
no matter how late,
it would be a good idea.

Silence

It can require at least a
second person
to whom one otherwise might listen or speak.
(Silence is more itself
if the two of you are in the same room.)

I haven't spoken
either of those sentences.
They tell me that when

persons is what we're talking about
(in the same or different rooms),

the Word was in the beginning.
If there'd been
before the Word
a first who might speak It,

there might not

yet have been a second.
Without a

second person,
(without
one second of time),

no word can be attended.

There was
God and the Word.
It's written that
these,

in the beginning,
were one.
John writes
that God was the Word.
He writes that the Word was

with God also.

That the Word was God and
with God—
this made

God
and the Word
two,
it separated them,

in the beginning,
so they could be together.
Without the Word and
God,
John writes,

there "was not anything
made that was made."

Before or
in the beginning
(almost as if, already, there was time),
the One Word promised that

the multiple might be,

existences plural.
According to the Word,
there might be
things in the mix with inexistence
(and inexistence,

still,
would much prevail).

God went ahead and said
Yes to things.
Right away

light was there,

and life,
and the life of persons. Persons
didn't understand.
(It goes without

saying about persons
that,
from the first,
the world
makes them its own.)

Brought to pass
after Elva and Jim said what if
anything to begin with,

and then, worldly,
touched,

my life's enjoined by the truth
that seventy-five
years ago,
in a town below the mountains,

I was nothing to speak of.

Her doctor told my mother she was expecting.
The man who sold my father our house

stayed on there in the room out back.
Old Mr. Berger. (He had a heavy accent and was kind.
I wasn't to call him Adolf.)

My mother's parents lived
three streets to the south.
Her father's last name,
Lee,
is in the middle of mine.

(I'm always

wanting to leave out my middle name.)
About my grandfather
I remember

only what I was told.
He outlived my infancy.
This means I heard him
say things that I understood.
I can't now

in memory
get any of it back.

I was told that he and I
liked one another,
and that he died.
Maybe I found myself

missing him
and couldn't do it.
I may have had to

rid me of him

(as I didn't Adolf Berger).
The passible

is what we're able to bear.
"I have many things to
say to you,"
John's Jesus said,

"but you can't hear them now."
I was three.
Was silence
all I could hear when someone told me
Bertram was dead? Had I been

able instead to let those
words in,

I'd have had to think
So that's what happens
just like that.

He may have asked me to remember him
the last time we talked.
Jesus bids
that He Himself
not be forgotten. Given to

Jesus in the Word is a stake
less ultimate
than what's written for each mortal in life/death.
Jesus is after all

Himself the Word,

and God.
(Jesus is God.)
Remembering
(aloud, with others) that what
happens for Him at the end must be

deathlike only,
I keep Christ

Jesus alive.
Bertram
I'm not

able to

or won't.
As thoroughly as my own embryonic
life is,
he's forgotten.

Immemorial,
deleted,

my grandfather's as

lost to me
as how it was
in silence

before I was born.
To my first inexistence
his death takes me back. As will be my
Nowhere-any-longer,

so was the Nowhere-yet.
Between two
inexistences,
the one
relation that's life.

Of What There Was First,

God's Word says that it
founds and exceeds what follows.
Existences are incomplete.
They need fixing. Bested

all the way through by what they might still be,
each has its garnered time and then that's
it for it,

there's no more to be heard from Bertram.
"So they
also may be One,
as We are,"
Christ begs God,

"keep those You've given Me
in Your Name."

The living are
(resistingly)
not

one yet.
A death at a time,
God makes us
equal in the Word,

forgiving
all of us

(save One)

our persons.
We were past the war.
At Sunday school in the second grade,
our teacher was patient with it when I broke the news
(even to me)

that I'd been born in China.
Out it had come.
My lie sat there with us
shamefaced,

huge,

for the rest of the hour.
I admitted having told it,

later,
to no one at home.
Unconfessed at home to
Elva was that
Elva was sick.

The grown-ups were her allies
as my mother kept
making herself up as on the mend.

She didn't have her little

breasts anymore.
Hadn't that been the problem right there?

All of us did our waiting.
With each next
doctor's visit, there'd be

word again
on how she was.
Watching when she was brought
home one afternoon from nights away,

I couldn't see as
dire and irreversible
her being lifted by my father from the car.
He wheeled her
inside,

where Florence and
I were.
Greeted,

my mother,

as she had to,
smiled.
Someone's lucky
quip right then let her

laughter at it
speak for us all.
Because our broken
Elva was among them,
no one said

"According to the greatness of Your
power,"

Lord,

"preserve those that are appointed to die."
It has been caused that
God is,
for some,
the Word

Without Whom There Is Nothing,
not empty

space,
even,
nor the thought of it
as having had to

be there first.
In the meted-out room
between them,

existing
things,

for some, are God's

address to God's clay.
When the Israelites
"saw the Voice,
they removed,
and stood afar off."

Flesh itself tells the unholy
they'll expire.
Those others who
receive God as the one true God

are promised they will live forever.
Over his child,
a father says "It just couldn't

end like that.
There has to be more."

When the existing thing God's Son is
dies and survives,
the cost to
some of us is every middle,

late or early death more final than His.

My faith's not what I'm told God wants it to be.
It can't attest
that I'll outlive my life.
Wishing
more for those I'm made to love and give up,

wishing more for me,
I need one
cranny in faith

not claimed by the Resurrection.
In the Word that's His Son,
each infinitely
lesser son is charged

to work God's will in loving.
Between

me
and "the least among us,"
my faith might find room.
As if I were myself
the inanimate, ignoring milieu,

I've failed to love
the one who's most afflicted
by the touch death keeps with life. Who in the world

is he, this "least"

or she?
It must be that I

miss her every day as one of the forgotten
blessings again
that I'd been urged to count and find the right
names for each night.

Wisdom

For the young man who would have
myrrh from a woman,
and cinnamon and aloes,

smoother than oil is her mouth. She flatters him with it.
Between her lips lies death.
The young man learns that as his bride he should instead have taken
Wisdom to him.
Wisdom is the words that figure her as

fear of the Lord.
She has seen Israel choose the ways of the oppressor.
The young men
Strangeness would claim

She instructs.
Wisdom pleads with them at the city gates that when

pride comes,

then comes shame.
Let a man meet rather
with a bear and her whelps
than with folly.
Withhold not

good from those to whom it is due.
The Lord's eyes are on

every place,
as on
Hell and destruction. Whose

order was it
that made the ends of the earth?
Who put clothes on the deep?
What is his name, and what is his

son's name,
if you can tell?

Wisdom can. Still a child,

she attended God when God had not yet
divided the waters.
It was no one but
God's to do
to divide what

isn't said
from what is.
If God was
male already,

Wisdom was not male.
(It may have been Wisdom's
difference from God that let God speak

good into being.)
Wisdom
was God's delight.
She was with him over the waters.
The still unformed

deep would have lasted
had God not given it form.
It made God tremble that His call for it to be
light there

would not let

night touch day. (There had to be room
between them
or they couldn't be what

God said they were.)
God and
Wisdom were two.
Day and night were two also.
Day gave it to be seen at once that

down was
and

up.
The deep had a face.
God's breath

hovered over it until there was

wind there instead.
The wind is in force in
many places over the earth's dry land.
Its going
on like that

is so it too can have extension
and still not be seen.

A door woke me.
It was having to
open and then flap shut against
the stable's north wall.

Some thuds were back-to-back. After others,

there'd be
a minute or more of only the wind.

The wind had become something the trees had had between
     them for
days now.
They'd showed to their tops that they'd be moved
only so much.
At the same time that it was many trees,

the night wind I was hearing them in was
one. (One has to be the number
God has
against the too-many-to-count.)

If it had a back to it
in those places how far north where
right then it was quiet,

the wind's broad front was as high as
just below God.
(That's where God starts to be a different
nothing than wind.)
If nothing's

around the wind to any of its sides,
Wisdom confides that
God's around all. Inside all God holds,

Wisdom's at the work of meaning for the faithful that there's
good to be had,
if God's heeded.
I wanted to be asleep so I wouldn't go on making

God up out of the wind.

Of Paul

And now abideth faith, hope, charity, these three . . .
1 COR 13:13

I

I am Paul's Jew or Gentile.
His hope is for such witness from me
that I will be his epistle.
He asks me to look into my faith.

How much of it I'll come to have has been dealt me.
I may make
too little of it
and be broken off
and fall. The law does not save. It must be by my

faith that I stand, and

faith comes by hearing.
That he might preach faith's word,

Paul set himself to know among us
only
Jesus Christ,

and him crucified.
As the Just One
died and made new
the unjust and the old,
so would Paul

each day die for me,

his blind and sleeping brother.
I'm not awake to God as the father of Jesus.
(God remains

God to me
and not a person.)
I fail Paul
when he asks me to see

heaven ahead as
surety that

my life now is only

on loan to God.
The time is short.
Paul prays that so much more might my

love abound
in knowledge and
judgment
that I will come to approve excellent things.

II

    Each morning this
July so far
(in back,

and from one house down),

I've overheard people I haven't seen.
I think there are three of them.
They have a dog that right now
can't cough something up,

and they have a pool.
They're always
mild with one another when they speak.
I'm favored that they
of course don't expect to hear

anything back from me. Reading,
listening,

I'm at my estimable

ease here
for any
familiar or new

next sound from outside.
I might
for the first time yet
claim that

Jesus is my redeemer.
My wife and

stepdaughter aren't here.
Nothing
either has heard me say would be as big.
But they love me.
I'd be making them take in from my

uncircumcised heart that it's
not what I feel.
It happens that
today

for my ears only

I can practice
"Jesus is my redeemer."
I knew what she was talking about
when someone I say I love
told me

I'd destroyed her life.
Later, I could hear the exaggeration in it.
She was talking about my not loving her enough

to keep my word.
Two nights after I broke it,

I was watching another Yankee rout in October,

I dropped off,
and when I
woke right away,

no one I could recognize as me
would do what I'd done.

In remorse,
a wrong that's been done takes up
one time in its doer,
another in the person wronged.
Redemption comes when the person no longer

hurts from that wrong.

III

A man who has a wife
sleeps as though he has none.
When sleep won't have him,

flesh makes him love

one only from among all
second persons,

female and male.
Dreamless sleep graces those in it
with an equity that
doesn't know sex.
The man bears to his wife in sleep unspoken

neighbor-love and no more,
he's made
no promises he can't take back.
Some promises are

faith-instilling.
They lend to the one who keeps them

an ease that turns

diseased when they fail.
It can happen that a wakeful man corrupts and does
something he hates.
He knows it all

day then: against the
shame he is
there ought to be a purge.
When at last at
night he falls off,

nothing he shares with other sleepers stops him from
loving himself.
(He must of course first love himself

if he's to love them.)

In the dark (with everyone
else asleep) about what's hurtful,

he isn't
missed now by the wife he's left
if she's asleep too.

Already two years ago
he missed
the woman who
should trust him to stay

in that same woman who still did.
He was sure she knew he loved her.
She'd go on knowing it
until he couldn't
make her have to see him anymore.

IV

What's sown is quickened
only if it dies.
We shall all be changed.
Passing away is the world's form.

To get
being right in the Pauline,

formed beings must be seen right through.
The force that
animates us shows as nothing at all.
When the man in one of Atget's
street-scenes moved,

he warped the exposure.
As by me my
own can't when I'm looking (except in a mirror),

his eyes can't be seen. Headless,

legless,
his shirtsleeves and vest dust the plate with clouds that can be

seen through
into the open dark door.
The forms of his
shoulders, though,
are back. They're

proprietary.
The place at 3 quai Conti is his,
The Little Dunkirk,
(kirk means a

church, of course,

the dun's
the bill collector,
dun's gray-brown,

this little
bill collector's
little
gray-brown church)
another

chamber
(like the camera)

a cabaret.
With him on watch there out front,
cider is for sale inside.

On the crossbar of the initials

IHS,
a child stands,
spear in hand,
above the entrance to

The Infant Jesus.
At The Little Bacchus,
the same naked

child again
smiles astride his cask.

The handle's

backside is the nearest form reflected in
The Grace of God's closed door that shows
behind the handle
first

the broad
trunk of a tree,
the rue Montmartre,
and curb.
The façade

across the street is freestone,
four stringcoursed bands of it extending

left out of view.
The wall they form is one of the two flanks an urban
trough needs.
Bringing to

naught by things that
are not
things that are,

Haussmann paid for his Godlike demolitions
with money no one had.
From the city's old
island center out,
shallow balconies line the block-long sides. The buildings'

height along them holds a uniform

3 to 2 ratio
to the width of the street.
Against
the big-as-day forms that stand there in accord,

a person
trues up his constructions.

Affording voids their solids,

the window piers
drafted to scale across each face show him at once both
entry

and entry barred.
Most
inner for him
is the self he's offscoured down to.
It does things he hates. Less strange than that self to him at times

are the outsides of all

load-bearing spans.
The corner rounded away has made room right and

left for what's there.
Integumented
people are.
All show
on his side of their planes and folds,

most are strangers to one another who bring
with them
into the streets

their wardings-off.
No one comes closer than an
arm's length here. No one's called out.
God knows

what's on their minds.
Persons

everywhere are

"with any as any with any."
In the stir there,
one among them charges herself

not to misrepresent.
To get least wrong
the character her
thinking him would turn him into,

she looks away from someone she sees.
She reads a sign for cotton
calico and flannel linings.
A billboard tells her "Summer in Dieppe."
Following each call for her trade,

a stranger gives his

flesh to reply to.
This one's
not on the make. Going
neighborly about his business,

he isn't
there
(she understands)
for being
looked to by her. Checking

back for him right away,
she sees he's moved on

out of her view.
Not that there aren't
others there to ignore.

The young man with two
sizable
and empty buckets.
Someone turbaned.
Sisters. An Alsatian

leashed to whom? It's the lot of them she's
with here,
here where they are.
Civil to let each of them be gone past

still nagged at by the call that anyone
alive here is

here to be served.
The person who shows as formed
conceals

inside his living aspect

life.
The unsubstitutable
life of someone.
It can't be seen

through to.
Another person's being
can't be got right.

There's also one's own.
It happens that the body proper

dies sometimes to its claims for itself. Sometimes

it serves. Whatever else its visible
form might be when it answers,
there are times
it's not one's own.
Who loves another has fulfilled the law.

When his body answers
Salonika and Corinth,
the Philippians, Galatia,

Rome,

Paul's
being in the Christ is

Paul's
as not
Paul's.
As those of an apostled
tentmaker,

his body's properties make it
Paul's.
Only thus is it also as
not Paul's

in those his letters beget.
So shall their seed be, who,

separated with Paul unto the gospel,
act in the hope
that no one lives or

dies to oneself.
His heirs in Christ hear being
itself said.
Paul offers how it

is with things,

he writes how things are.
We're beings who have about them
the savor of
death unto death.
As it's forever back into it that all

ruined beings go,
being is that from out of which
one's prospects as a being
come to the fore. Life

happens to you out of the blue.
You're born to have it be that

others are there already as your lookouts.
When she wasn't a
baby anymore,
her father told her
she must have had a halo around her whole body,

they loved her so much. (He'd said she

"must" have had it.
That meant the nimbus they were sure of wasn't
formed to be seen.)

More than once
she'd watched clouds
stack so over a sweep of country
that,
scapelike too,

they had the look of matter
deep with its own coordinates and darks.
To no horizon,
the clouds had been stretched

into themselves from
sky.
Each form

(too late at it already)

giving
place right away,

the passings showed how
anything she sees
screens over what
supplies it

and then takes it back.
When she was
ten one day at the hospital,

her mother
looked at her and struggled to

ask about school.

Coffined was how she saw her next.
On that day,
of just her mother and her,
she herself was the one who could see
to walk across the room and

do that
when her father asked
did she

want to touch her mother.
She should have wanted to.
Maybe it was good to have done.
She touched the right

cheek a little
and thought her mother had for
days now been cloud.
Something she couldn't really
know about her

she knew:

her mother wasn't in heaven.
After that,

there'd been the years her father wasn't
sick yet.
She doesn't know who's living now
inside the third-floor windows that were his.
They're people she doesn't look for when she stands out front,

she might be seen

down on the street
outside
by someone not her father.
(If she herself weren't

visible anymore, she couldn't
see he's not here.)

In the measure that she trusts
all persons are
(as Paul is) held "in Christ,"

a person's
loved improbability for someone else brings
weeping when it's lost,
but also

isn't wept for,

Christ warranting it as saved.
Against death's having
Hagar's son outright,

and Sarah's,
Jesus said
"Before
Abraham was,
I am,"

for the sons and daughters inside
Jesus alive,

this promised fastness of a

place-not-timed.
Unexposed "in
Christ" there,
contained,

the mourned are
yet in that life assented to
by any for whom

nothing's
outside Christ,

not the unborn,
not any person's
death, even, which if
outside Christ
would mean a life we're

ditched by too soon.
Death can be the last thing given.
It can perfect

timelessly
a Now that lasts.
Paul wants us to know the last thing
he was given was the

Christ in him
whom he himself was in.
For himself
first he prayed to
"Let this mind be in you which was

also in

Christ Jesus,
who thought it not plunder to be

equal with God,
but made himself of
no reputation."
Only when he'd made his God-form

mortal for a while
and died
could Jesus be reputed

always to live.
Risen from the dead, Jesus

preached again.
Five hundred people heard him.
It was said of Jesus that that was how it was.
If Jesus spoke from his
body again after he died,

it couldn't be that it was only

said that he did.
The Resurrection either

was or was not.
Only if it was not can it be
fabled as true.

So exalted

is no one else's death.
Storied for millennia as
life-giving,
Jesus may have

more than somewhat died.
Death
faces people down.
If the deity isn't
itself death,

God
nevertheless,
that He might give all life,

takes all.
God too is one as singularly as any person's one

death is. "For
Thy sake is it, God, that we are killed
all the day long."
God's extravagant
Word to him about rescue

Jesus took to the cross. If he lived

abandonment there,
able when he said
"forsaken"
not to know he'd be saved,

how much blame is there in Jesus's
"Why . . . ?"
The last guest
Jesus could receive was
God, the Taker. For all

Jesus could tell,
God was coming to stay.
Is God's face death's?

In a late summoning that says God's
Jesus's still,
he twice calls out "My God . . ."
to his desolating Father-stranger.

(Love's

hidden from sometimes
by those it dismays.

It can outlast
its being turned back
unacknowledged.)
Dying can be

lived through.
Death can't,
and sometimes
neither can love.
Did Jesus

love God when he died?
God
may not have made him have to.

If God's last name is

It-Has-Been-Caused-That . . . ,
the ellipsis's Ys and Zs can to the end of them be

rife with impurpose,
utter,
and at each turn
yours.
"What do you

have,"

Paul asks,
"that you did not receive?"
Little that she's not already been made
subject to

as given
and must lose.

Composure will stay
on for a while more
as not yet plight.
Just past the inelastic

middle of it,
each point in time she comes by
chafes away
toward her last
instant-to-come. Before that flash that's

the end,
never will she have had as much and

little to do. Death's so
run through in time by each life's fullness
that it takes life in.
She'll have given up time itself

when it was time.
If the temporal were less an
issue, so would

God be. When time
isn't anymore,

then only will she
know and be known by God.
It's intelligible for now
to wish God a person.
Of persons,

only the most bestial would have your

death be the end.
It's been caused that there will be no
end soon

to how long she'll go on being someone who'd lived.
Along with God,
she'll be
insensible and ever-during. Busy

after her will be the mutual lives and deaths of every
smallest thing else.

Pasts

I tell myself
I'll eventually have had
three. The first

ended when I was born.
I couldn't have known
before then that
down the ages
there'd been

Prague in the 1820s,
primogeniture,

and Lewis and Clark.

On the Victrola from early in my
second past,
Fred Waring and the Pennsylvanians.
"Not a creature was stirring"

in our post–Pearl Harbor blackout.
The block warden was my father. Nightly,
he went house to house.
I did my best to believe him:
the Japanese couldn't hear us from their planes.

The things I remember spoil me.
I know I can't keep making them turn

up now
for years and years more.
Wanting them to,
I construct as an impossible

third past
my
over-before-I-know-it-

if-never-quite-

here-yet
last moment ever.
May I be asleep when it happens.
It might matter

less then
that I can't be on the back

side of it

to make it a past.
Finding their ways to
fable sometimes

are futures that will never be present.
Into my conjured
third past,
I'm disposed
to bring

and be brought by
God.

Immune to human overlay that would
grant God pardon,
God is a concept larger than the oblivion I expect.
God is

thanks I can't fail to give
for lives that must be completed.
Death annuls me only if it's
my terms that are willed.
I pray someone

else's will
for whom prayer's always what it's
often for me.

Hidden

In dogma
is the secret that renders God unconditioned,

on one condition.
"If you are not My people,
I am not your God."
As fashioned by His people's witness,

a made thing,
God,
condemns the made things graven

images are. Inscribed as born

wittingly of Himself,
God is
(so to speak)
that Father
abler than the most sovereign

earthly father to make
all things good.
God the Father is conceived as

for us.
Purposive,
stewarding,
benign,

He covenants our living on.
"Written in

continuance" in His Book
before they took form
were the parts of our fitful bodies.
As if what's
given with the world is

life only,

life,
and not
(along with it,
in time) at last, life's needful withdrawal,

God's said to let the truthful
keep their lives forever if they swear God
does what He says.
These are the portions: either
I'll outlast death

or it me.
Little matter which

if it's the avowed

God I'm given up to.
That I'm settled in the finite is what's true instead.
Living is a good I don't want stopped

even for the saved.
I'm beholden to it all the way that,
in its one chance each with me and others,
death hasn't used itself
up yet. Mine affords me another day

hours before it's light. Along with the caused
things outside that I can't see, I'm here
ahead of myself again
toward that coupling with the ground

when "I am poured out like water."

Death's still to be heard from at its least reserved.

Under its breath it primes me to pay up and look pleasant.

*

*

*

*

*

*

*

*

*

*

*

Acknowledgments

Earlier versions of these poems have appeared in *The New York Times*, *The Cincinnati Review*, *The Cortland Review*, and *Ploughshares*.